ENTERTAINMENT

SCREEN, STAGE & STARS

Series Editor:
David Salariya was born in Dundee, Scotland, where he studied illustration and printmaking, concentrating on book design in his post-graduate year. He later completed a further post-graduate course in art education at Sussex University. He has illustrated a wide range of books on botanical, historical and mythical subjects. He has designed and created many new series of children's books for publishers worldwide. In 1989, he established his own publishing company, The Salariya Book Company Ltd.

Author:
Jacqueline Morley is a graduate of Somerville College, Oxford. She has taught English and history, and now works as a freelance translator and writer. She has written historical fiction and non-fiction for children, and has a particular interest in the history of everyday life. She has also written *Clothes* in the *Timelines* series, and is the author of two books in the *How Would You Survive?* series.

Consultant:
Robert Gordon is a Senior Lecturer in Drama at Goldsmith's College, London. He has worked as a professional actor and director, and his writing includes *Tom Stoppard: Text and Performance*. He has also written books and articles on British theater, and his plays *Waterloo Road* and *Red Earth* have been performed in London.

Series Editor	David Salariya
Senior Editor	Ruth Nason
Consultant	Robert Gordon
Artists	Mark Bergin
	Ronald Coleman
	Lee Elliot
	Nick Hewetson
	John James
	Sarah Kensington
	Mark Peppé
	Carolyn Scrace

First published in the United States in 1994
by Franklin Watts

Franklin Watts
95 Madison Avenue
New York, N.Y. 10016

© The Salariya Book Company Ltd MCMXCIII

Printed in Belgium

Library of Congress Cataloging-in-Publication Data

Morley, Jacqueline.
    Entertainment / by Jacqueline Morley.
        p.   cm. —(Timelines)
    Includes index.
    Summary: Traces the history of such forms of entertainment as drama, dance, opera, and film.
        ISBN 0-531-14311-2 (lib. bdg.)—0-531-15710-5 (pbk.)
    1. Performing arts—History—Juvenile literature. 2. Theater—History—Juvenile literature. [1. Performing arts—History. 2. Theater—History.] I. Title. II. Series: Timelines (Franklin Watts, inc.)
PN1581.M67 1994
790.dc—20
93-4826
CIP AC

Artists
Mark Bergin, p 31-32, p 36-37;
Ronald Coleman p 10-11, p 20-21, p 26-27;
Lee Elliot p 18-19; **Nick Hewetson**, p 24-25, p 28-29, p 30-31; **John James**, p 14-15, p 16-17;
Sarah Kensington p12-13, p 40-41,
Mark Peppé, p 6-7, p 8-9, p 38-39;
Carolyn Scrace, p 22-23, p 34-35, p 42-43.

TIMELINES
ENTERTAINMENT

SCREEN, STAGE & STARS

Written by
JACQUELINE MORLEY

Created & Designed by
DAVID SALARIYA

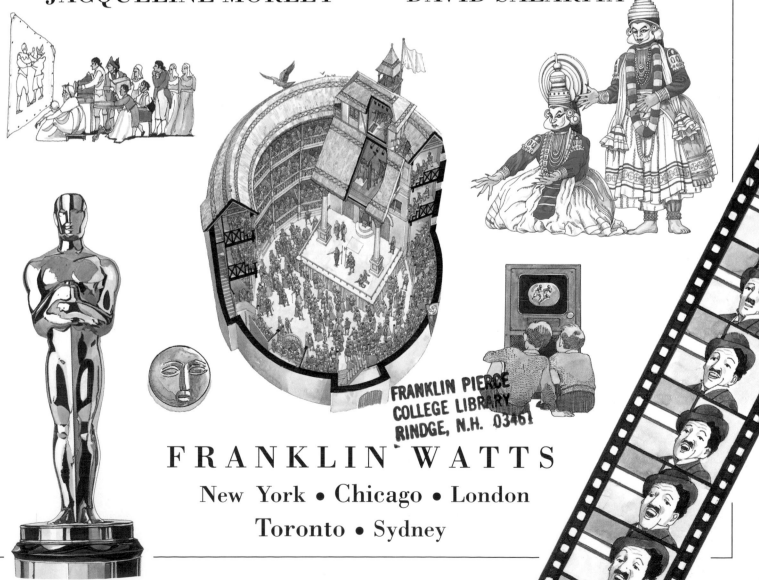

FRANKLIN WATTS
New York • Chicago • London
Toronto • Sydney

CONTENTS

△ SOUTH AFRICAN bushman painting of an animal dance.

▽ DANCING in Papua New Guinea to honor a god.

▽ WILDCAT MASK worn by Cherokee Indians to stalk turkeys. Acting the wildcat magically gave them its skills.

THE BEGINNINGS

WHAT IS ENTERTAINMENT? Something you want when you are bored? Today, entertainment tends just to happen, like television, without any effort. Someone else does the work. And although you may become absorbed in a play or in dancing at a disco, you may not feel that it is an essential part of life, and it is just for amusement.

In the past it was quite different. If we take a backward glance at the history of entertainment, we might be startled by its magical and dangerous origins. Dance and song are basic human activities, used by our ancestors for a purpose. They danced and sang to their gods when they begged for good hunting, for rain, or for protection from evil spirits. This was a serious and sacred business, and remains so for primitive societies.

◁ ANCIENT EGYPTIANS, dressed as friendly household gods, taking part in a sacred dance.

▽ ANCIENT EGYPTIAN professional dancers and musicians, around 1400 B.C. Performers like these were hired to play in wealthy homes. By this time people had begun to enjoy music and dancing for their own sakes, as well as using them as a way of speaking to the gods.

△ PERFORMERS of sacred dances and songs might take acting roles, imitating animals or celebrating the deeds of gods. In ancient Egypt (after 3000 B.C.), at great religious festivals, the priests re-enacted tales of the gods. This was the beginning of drama being presented to an audience to arouse a response.

ANCIENT GREECE

△ A CHORUS representing warriors on horseback, shown on a 6th-century Greek vase.

▷ THE CHORUS performed on a circle of ground at the foot of a hill. The hillside was stepped to seat the audience.

DRAMA IN ANCIENT GREECE, as in Egypt, grew out of religious ceremonies. Every year people danced and sang to honor Dionysus, the god of wine and fertility. In Athens, this annual festival included a competition for the best song. The songs were chanted by a group of men, the *chorus*. In 534 B.C. Thespis, a priest of Dionysus, won the prize with a brilliant novelty. He introduced a performer who exchanged comments with the leader of the chorus, producing the first actor and dialogue in the history of theater. On each day of the festival of Dionysus people flocked to watch the chorus perform in a circular area called the *orchestra*.

△ THE ORCHESTRA had an altar to Dionysus in the center. Actors entered from a building known as the *skene*. The acting area before it was the *proscenium*. Backgrounds were often painted on the *skene*, the source of our word "scenery."

◁ A PROCESSIONAL wagon representing Dionysus in a ship.

▷ AN ACTOR with the mask he will put on. All actors were men and wore masks.

▷ A TRAGIC MASK. Each mask established a character's sex, age, and feelings.

THE GREEKS invented three types of drama – tragedies that dealt with noble themes such as honor and bravery; satyric plays that were sarcastic and mocking; and comedies full of clowning and farce. *Left*, farce scene on a vase. *Right*, how the same scene was acted, by traveling players on a portable stage.

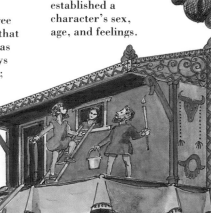

7

ANCIENT ROME

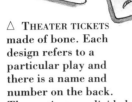

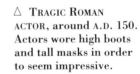

THE ROMANS COPIED Greek theater, but whereas the Greeks had gone to the theater to listen to ideas about their society and its conflicts, most Romans at the height of the Empire (1st century A.D.) went there because they had nothing better to do. Many Romans were unemployed, though the state supported them. They wanted entertainment to help them to forget their difficult lives – violent drama, comedy and "mime" (a mixture of acrobatics and farce). Productions became more and more spectacular. In a play called *A House on Fire* a real house and its contents were burned on stage; the actors kept whatever they rescued from the flames. When a character had to die, the actor's place was taken by a criminal, who was killed on stage.

△ THEATER TICKETS made of bone. Each design refers to a particular play and there is a name and number on the back. The seating was divided into named sections with numbered seats.

△ MASK OF A SLAVE in a comedy.

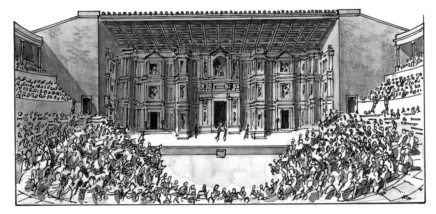

△ A ROMAN THEATER of the 1st century A.D., based on remains at Orange in southern France, then the Roman province of Gaul.

Most theaters were huge, seating about 20,000 people. The religious origins of drama had been forgotten. There was no altar, and no chorus.

The stage was now the focus of attention. It was roofed and had an elaborate rear wall suggesting buildings, with several entrances for the actors.

△ TRAGIC ROMAN ACTOR, around A.D. 150. Actors wore high boots and tall masks in order to seem impressive.

▽ THE THEATER at Orange had a colonnaded courtyard, where the audience could stroll – an idea copied from Greece. Next to it was a *circus*.

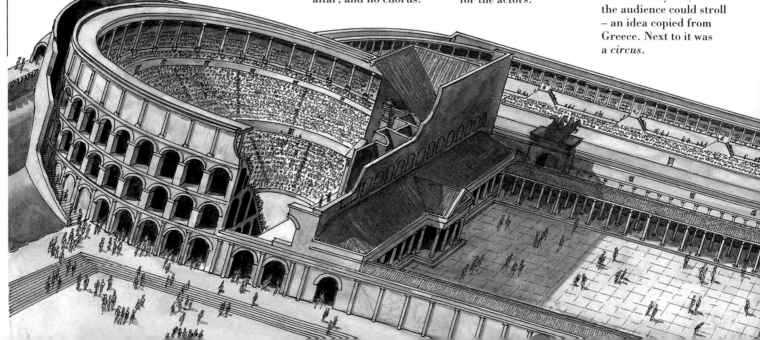

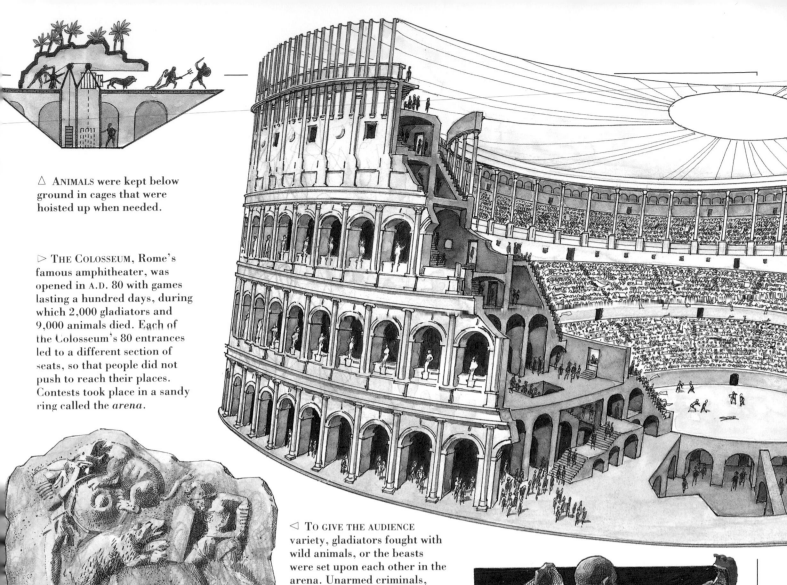

△ ANIMALS were kept below ground in cages that were hoisted up when needed.

▷ THE COLOSSEUM, Rome's famous amphitheater, was opened in A.D. 80 with games lasting a hundred days, during which 2,000 gladiators and 9,000 animals died. Each of the Colosseum's 80 entrances led to a different section of seats, so that people did not push to reach their places. Contests took place in a sandy ring called the *arena*.

◁ TO GIVE THE AUDIENCE variety, gladiators fought with wild animals, or the beasts were set upon each other in the arena. Unarmed criminals, and later Christians, were sent in to be torn to pieces by them.

Since the 6th century B.C. the Romans had celebrated religious festivals and great occasions with sports called *ludi* (games). These were originally gymnastic events, or chariot races run at breakneck speed around a U-shaped track called a *circus*. During the 3rd century B.C. gladiator combats (fights to the death) became part of the games, and were soon the biggest attraction. Special circular buildings, called *amphitheaters*, were designed to give the best view to the largest number of people. Slaves and misfits became professional gladiators to win rich prizes.

When Christianity became the official religion of Rome in the 4th century, such contests were banned. In the 6th century, theaters were also banned, because mime players poked fun at religion.

△ EACH GLADIATOR was a specialist in one of several styles of fighting. The man on the left has a net to fling over his opponent and a trident to spear him with once he is entangled.

A wounded gladiator could beg the crowd for mercy. If he had fought well they might give a thumbs up sign to spare him, but if not they turned their thumbs down and called out to have his throat cut.

CHINA

THE THEATER OF THE EAST, like that of the west, has its origins in religion. As early as 700 B.C. entertainers performed at Chinese religious festivals. In around A.D. 720, the emperor Ming Huang set up an actors' training school in the Pear Garden of the Imperial Park. Dance-dramas were performed in temples and at festivals. Permanent theaters appeared in the 13th century, and regional styles developed. Since the 19th century Peking opera has been the favorite style. Its traditional characters – tyrants, demons, young girls, gods and goddesses– enact well-known tales from history and legend.

△ A TRADITIONAL moon lute, named after its large round sound box. Music from an orchestra of seven or eight players is an essential part of Chinese theater.

△ A CHINESE ACTOR'S makeup. In the earliest dance-dramas actors wore masks. Later they painted their faces to look like masks. In Peking opera each actor uses colors and designs that, by tradition, express the character portrayed. A white-faced character is cowardly or cunning, a blue one ferocious, a red-faced one loyal and courageous. Gods have gold faces; devils green ones. A combination of colors indicates a complex character. Costumes are elaborate but there is little in the way of scenery or props. A table is a bridge; an oar represents a ship. The actors use movement to express what is going on. Each character has its own pattern of gestures.

△ AN OPEN-AIR THEATER. A carpet is the acting area, with props on a table behind it.

▽ SWORD DANCERS in Peking opera. Events are shown symbolically. A sword dance represents a battle. An actor covered by a blue flag drowns in the sea.

Peking opera tells its stories through a spectacular combination of dialogue, gymnastics, dance, and song. When the Communists took over China in 1949 they encouraged realistic Western-type plays, but the public refused to give up Peking opera, and official policy had to be changed.

JAPAN

JAPAN PRESERVES ancient theatrical traditions. The oldest is Bugaku, a warrior dance based on Asian court dances, brought to Japan over a thousand years ago and now forgotten elsewhere. It is performed at the imperial court and at shrines. In the 14th century a disciplined form of drama called Noh was created to entertain nobles and warriors whose code of conduct forbade the expression of emotions. Events and feelings were hinted at. Kabuki theater, a much livelier mixture of story, song, and dance, was developed in the 17th century. Noh and Kabuki are still very popular.

△ MASK OF A DEMON of jealousy. Only certain families know the skills of making Noh masks. Actors believe that when they put on a mask its spirit enters them.

△ BUGAKU DANCER dressed as a medieval imperial guard. The majestic dances are performed on platforms in temple courtyards.

▽ NOH PLAYS are still performed according to instructions written in A.D. 1400. No dramatic action takes place on stage.

Music pavilion (dressing room).

Passageway

Musicians.

Audience.

Noh stage.

Chorus.

Audience.

△ MUSIC accompanies the chanted speech of a Noh character, who tells of past events.

▷ THE MAIN CHARACTER in a Noh play is masked and wears a splendid costume. A second actor asks him questions to prompt the narrative.

△ IN NOH PLAYS all actions and emotions are stylized. A drooping head and raised hand mean weeping; a slight movement of the sleeve conveys longings of love.

◁ A 19TH-CENTURY Kabuki theater. The revolving stage was a Kabuki invention.

△ KABUKI ACTORS are all men. They are trained in the tradition from childhood.

▷ THESE ACROBATIC DANCERS from a modern Japanese ballet are very different from the strict traditions of Noh and Kabuki.

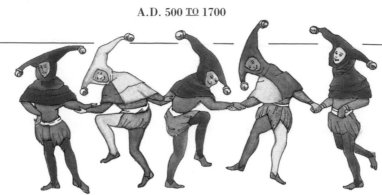

◁ DANCING JESTERS, from a Flemish manuscript of around 1340. Since Roman times, a cap with long ears, like a donkey's, had been the costume of the fool.

POPULAR TRADITIONS

WHAT HAPPENED to the well-loved comedy characters established by the Romans – the forgetful old man, the swaggering soldier, and the innocent young girl – when the Christian authorities closed the theaters? Of course, they were not forgotten. These characters are stock types that appeal to something basic in human nature. From the Dark Ages onward, street entertainers all over Europe performed the old jokes, as clowns, dancers, ballad singers, acrobats, and puppeteers. They kept alive the skills and technical tricks of the theater.

△ A VIKING FAMILY of about A.D. 900 gather round to listen to a story. Storytelling is the oldest form of simple amusement, unconnected with religious worship.

△ A MEDIEVAL JUGGLER on stilts. Wandering street entertainers – wrestlers, tight-rope walkers, people with dancing bears and monkeys – were familiar figures at medieval fairs.

◁ A TROUPE of 14th-century mummers who are celebrating a wedding. The custom of dancing in animal disguises is ancient and found all over the world.

In winter time, mummers came banging on doors, demanding food, drink, or money in return for masked dances or simple plays that often featured a shaggy wild man dressed in green. The players were local people in disguise. It was thought to be unlucky to turn them away without hospitality. This folk custom had its roots in old pagan ceremonies held to banish winter and make crops sprout.

◁ THIS 15TH-CENTURY woodcut shows musicians dressed as fools serenading a lady. She does not seem to like their music.

▷ 15TH-CENTURY MUMMERS perform a play in the hall of a manor house.

Horacio. Pulcinella. Il Dottore. Lucretia. Pantalone. Pierrot. Harlequin. Scaramouche.

△ HARLEQUIN was a favorite character, crafty, witty, and acrobatic. Originally he was dressed in patches to show that he was poor. By the 17th century, this had become the costume with regular diamond-shaped checks.

In about 1550 the Commedia dell'Arte, a type of traveling theater, emerged in Italy. Its characters – Harlequin, the clever servant; Pantalone, the miserly old merchant; and Columbine, the coy servant girl – were old comic types that had taken on new life. The witty dialogue, made up on the spot, included jibes at authority and indecent jokes, and the action consisted of practical jokes, farcical plots, acrobatics, and knock-about fun. From 1550 to 1650 the Italian actors of the Commedia were as popular with kings and queens as with peasants, not only in Italy but in France, Spain, Holland, Germany, and England. Its heyday was past by 1700, but its characters lived on in other forms of entertainment, in puppetry, ballet, and pantomime.

▷ A COMMEDIA DELL' ARTE leather mask. All the comic characters wore half-masks. The plots usually told a story about a pair of young lovers. These characters, and others like the handsome Horacio and the lady Lucretia, were not masked.

▷ THE TRAVELING STAGE had a rear curtain, and often two side buildings of painted boards. These provided entrances, and a window used for comic business, rather like the ancient Greek stage on page 7.

◁ THE CHARACTER of Pierrot was developed by the French version of the Commedia dell'Arte. He grew into a gentle, wistful figure. 19th-century seaside entertainers often dressed as Pierrot.

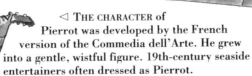

△ PANTALONE rides a makeshift horse in an attempt to woo the lady Lucretia.

▷ COMMEDIA DELL'ARTE players arriving in town. They traveled in their costumes, partly as advertisement and partly because the actors carried their stage roles into real life.

RELIGIOUS DRAMA

THE CHRISTIAN CHURCH, which had banned the theater, was itself the cause of its rebirth. In the early Middle Ages priests began to act out little scenes during church services, to bring alive the story and teachings of Christ. These began as short episodes with very few characters. On Easter Sunday, for example, priests dressed as the three Marys visited a mock-up of Christ's tomb, where an angel would tell them of the Resurrection. The idea was so effective that soon several scenes were acted, using temporary settings, or *mansions*, in various parts of the church. Before long there were so many actors and such large crowds that the churches could not hold them, and the plays began to be acted outside, in front of the church door, and eventually out along the streets.

By now so many character parts were needed that local people were called in to help. They introduced their own ideas, some taken from the street entertainers and some from the ancient mummers' plays and pagan festivals. The themes remained religious, but comic incidents were often woven in. The Christmas shepherds became involved in sheep stealing, and Mrs. Noah turned into a vixen who boxed Noah's ears.

△ WOOD CARVING showing Christ driving out the moneylenders, a scene from a 15th-century Easter play performed in Vienna.

◁ AN EASTER PLAY is performed in a medieval cathedral. The mansions between the pillars of the nave represent places such as Bethlehem, Nazareth, Herod's palace and the Mount of Olives. The congregation follows as the actors move from place to place. The priest playing Christ has rushed down the steps of the mansion representing the temple at Jerusalem, to scatter the moneylenders. In the center of the nave stands the throne from which Pilate will judge Christ, and in the distance two actors wait to play the sleeping soldiers as Christ rises from the sepulcher. To the right is hell's mouth, full of demons who will delight the audience with antics and horrible faces.

△ A PRIEST hands a player his devil's mask. The Devil was played for laughs, and became a great favorite with the audiences.

As the plays grew more elaborate, each guild of a town became responsible for one scene, often related to its trade. The bakers performed the Last Supper, the boat-builders Noah's Ark, and so on. By the 15th century, mansions filled the market squares on church festival days, and they were put on carts, called pageants, that took the plays to audiences through the town.

▽ A 15TH-CENTURY pageant cart. Lowering an actor from the sky is an old theatrical trick. The ancient Greeks had used it.

▷ THE PAGEANT has halted before an audience grouped around a platform that is level with its stage. The cutaway shows the lower story, for props, machinery, and costume changes. It is hidden by a curtain all around, but devils can spring up from it through a trapdoor.

THE GLOBE THEATER

BY THE MIDDLE of the 16th century, the professional entertainers who toured the fairs were beginning to form small companies to perform plays. They traveled from town to town, carrying their gear in a cart, and were looked upon with some suspicion by "respectable" people. In Italy such touring theater companies produced the Commedia dell'Arte (see page 13).

In 16th-century England, and in London especially, there was a great appetite for plays. The better companies were supported financially by great lords and toured under their name. In 1576 one of the Earl of Leicester's men, an actor called James Burbage, decided to build a permanent theater. He modeled it on the type of wooden building used for bear-baiting shows, with tiers of seats, sheltered by a thatched roof, surrounding a ring that was open to the sky. It was named "The Theater."

△ A COMPANY of traveling players have set up their stage in the courtyard of an inn.

△ A DAY AT THE GLOBE. Dawn. Londoners are just beginning to stir. On the south bank of the Thames the early light reveals the tall round shapes of the Globe theater, *left*, and to the right its rival, the Rose.

△ 7 A.M. Rain! The manager fears he must cancel today's play. The audience won't want to get soaked.

△ 10 A.M. Fine again. A stage hand hoists a flag from the theater's turret to signal that the play will go on.

Burbage's scheme was so successful that by 1600, London had several theaters. His son Richard was the leading actor of the day, and was fortunate to have William Shakespeare as a member of his company, the Lord Chamberlain's Men. In 1598 the company built a theater called the Globe on the south bank of the Thames. There are no surviving pictures of the original inside of the Globe, which was burned down in 1613 and rebuilt in 1614.

Spain also had great playwrights and avid theatergoers at this time. The interior of Madrid's first theater, of 1579, recorded in a surviving plan, had much in common with the English type.

△ 2 P.M. A trumpeter blows from a roof platform to announce the start of the play.

△ 2:15 P.M. In the dressing room behind the stage, actors practice while waiting to go on.

△ IN THE TOP ROOF-SPACE stagehands turn a winch that lowers the actor through the roof onto the stage. This mechanism was invented by the ancient Greeks.

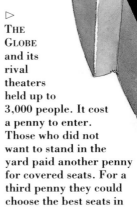

▷ THE GLOBE and its rival theaters held up to 3,000 people. It cost a penny to enter. Those who did not want to stand in the yard paid another penny for covered seats. For a third penny they could choose the best seats in the first two tiers.

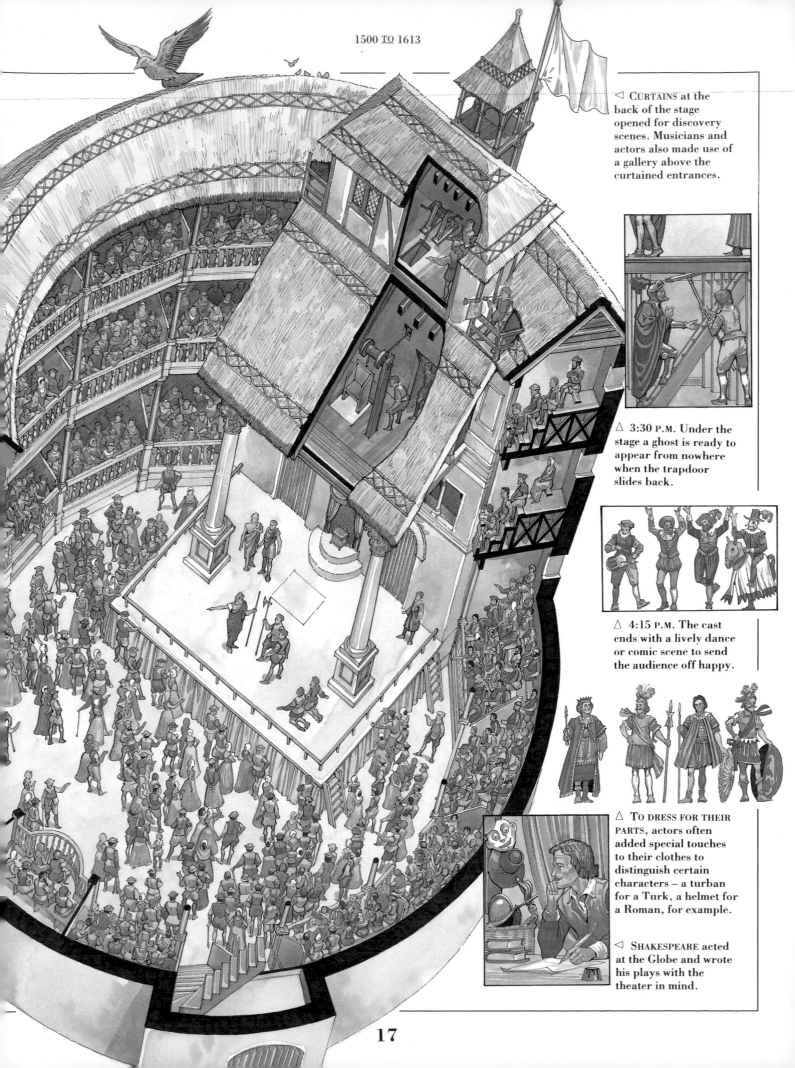

◁ CURTAINS at the back of the stage opened for discovery scenes. Musicians and actors also made use of a gallery above the curtained entrances.

△ 3:30 P.M. Under the stage a ghost is ready to appear from nowhere when the trapdoor slides back.

△ 4:15 P.M. The cast ends with a lively dance or comic scene to send the audience off happy.

△ TO DRESS FOR THEIR PARTS, actors often added special touches to their clothes to distinguish certain characters – a turban for a Turk, a helmet for a Roman, for example.

◁ SHAKESPEARE acted at the Globe and wrote his plays with the theater in mind.

△ DANCERS performing the Bharata Nhatyam, from a carving on a 10th-century Hindu temple.

▽ KATHAK dancing girls entertaining guests at the court of the Emperor Akbar, from a 16th-century miniature. They are celebrating the birth of the future Emperor Jahangir in A.D. 1568.

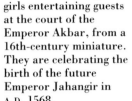

△ KATHAK is strongly rhythmic, with rapid turning and foot tapping to the sound of drums and wind instruments.

▽ A DANCE INSTRUCTOR guides a pupil through the movements of the Bharata Nhatyam. The ancient tradition is still very much alive.

INDIA

INDIAN THEATRICAL TRADITIONS are perhaps the oldest of all. It seems likely that temple dance-drama started in India, and some scholars believe its beginnings may pre-date Athenian drama by as much as two thousand years. From India it spread to China and southeast Asia.

The Bharata Nhatyam is a Hindu temple dance from southern India that goes back to the 5th century B.C. It uses a sign language of gestures and glances to express spiritual meaning. Kathakali, by contrast, is a north Indian dance of later origin. It began as an entertainment at Muslim courts after the Mongol invasions of A.D. 1260 on.

Indian languages have no separate words for "dance" and "drama." Later dance plays, which developed from the temple dances, were based on stories of the Hindu gods and were still regarded as religious performances.

▷ KATHAKALI ACTORS are all male. Kathakali, a 17th-century form of dance-drama, is still seen today. It is acted outdoors at night. Singers chant the story and dialogue, which the dancers "speak" with their eyes and hands, using over 500 hand gestures. Rice-paper shapes are stuck around their faces and a crushed seed in each eye turns the whites red.

AFRICA

IN AFRICA COMMUNITIES still join together in dance and song to celebrate important human experiences – birth, coming of age and death. In west and central Africa official storytellers called *griots* were an honored hereditary caste. Their songs preserved the history, wisdom, and humor of their people. Villagers still gather to listen to the *griot*.

Drama can be a powerful means of spreading ideas. African nations have inherited many problems, and today drama, brought to the people by touring groups, is a practical method of exploring these problems and discussing ideas.

African music traveled to the New World with slaves shipped to the plantations. There, in the late 19th century, its special rhythms produced blues and jazz (see page 40).

△ RUANDA WARRIORS (of east central Africa) celebrate the strength of their tribe in around 1900. Their intricate dance is performed before their chief in the courtyard of the royal palace.

Tambourine.   Shawm.   Drum.   Tambourine.

◁ ALGERIAN street musicians playing a shawm, two tambourines, and a drum.

▽ THESE JOHANNESBURG WORKERS are performing *Ngoma*, a Zulu group dance with song. They dance for their own satisfaction, not for an audience, expressing their defiance through symbolic warrior gestures.

△ BANTU MUSICIANS. Africa has a larger variety of drums than any other continent. "Talking" drums originated in Africa. Squeezing the thongs on their sides produces changes of pitch that imitate the sound of speech.

▽ JOHN KANI AND WINSTON NTSHOMA in the 1974 production of *Sizwe Bansi Is Dead*, a play they created with the playwright Athol Fugard, that explores black suffering under apartheid in South Africa.

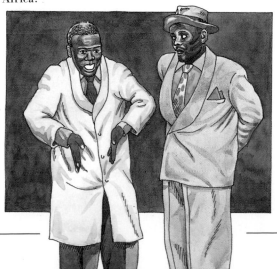

PRINCELY ENTERTAINMENTS

△ A 15TH-CENTURY knight in tournament armor galloping to meet his opponent. He tries to topple him from his horse with the lance.

▽ AN ARCHDUKE and courtiers enter Brussels in 1596, escorted by city dignitaries.

MEDIEVAL AND RENAISSANCE kings and princes organized luxurious entertainments not for pleasure alone, but also because in those days a ruler was expected to be surrounded by costly display, pageantry, and glitter. This showed others how powerful he was.

Tournaments, or mock battles, were a favorite pastime. Only the nobility took part in them; the local people were allowed to watch. In the early Middle Ages tournaments had been a risky form of war training, but by about 1400 they had become festive games governed by elaborate rules. They lasted several days, each day ending with feasts and dances.

When kings were crowned, paid state visits, or returned victorious from war, they entered cities in extravagant processions. Magnificent triumphal arches were put up in the streets, and musicians or actors waited on temporary stages to play music or recite poems of greeting along the route. Onlookers lined the streets.

▽ A TRIUMPHAL ARCH, one of a series that greeted James I when he entered London in 1604. They were made of scaffolding, canvas, and boards, and were painted and gilded.

▽ SOME OF THE DECORATIONS were real people. As King James approached, Fame, at the top, blew a trumpet, the musicians played, and the Good and Bad Forces seated around the Fountain of Virtue had a fight. Good won, of course, and the Fountain flowed with wine.

△ THIS DRAGON FLOAT appeared in a parade in Brussels in 1615, together with floats with religious themes. Pageantry gets its name from the pageants used for religious plays. The techniques for staging big street shows were the same whatever the theme. We use them today for parades.

Fifteenth-century rulers enlivened the formality of palace life by entertaining their guests with spectacular surprises. At banquets, pies were likely to burst open to reveal musicians, and between the courses floats would enter carrying maidens running away from ogres, or wicked knights issuing challenges. In France and Italy, a favorite pastime was for courtiers to dress up in rich and fantastic costumes and masks and to perform dances. By the 17th century these performances, known as *masques*, had become very elaborate, with songs, dances, scenery, and a linking plot. They became popular all over Europe as an aristocratic entertainment.

▷ A COURTIER dancing as a clockmaker in an entertainment at the court of Louis XIV in 1690. The courtiers and the king enjoyed dressing up, though in a most stately way.

▷ AN ENTERTAINMENT staged in 1581 at the court of Henry III of France. There were three set scenes: a wood on the right, a cloud with musicians on the left, and the garden of Circe the enchantress at the far end. The courtiers glided in on floats, sparkling with lights, which one by one circled the hall, pausing for a song or recital in front of the king. Each float was linked to a simple plot telling a story about Circe. This event was called a *ballet* and ended in a dance.

△ HORSEMEN take part in an open-air spectacle put on for Louis XIV in 1662.

INDOOR THEATER

THE ITALIANS were great innovators in the theater. In the late 15th century, Renaissance enthusiasm for ancient Greek and Roman art led them to revive classical plays and try to recreate ancient theaters. Theater designers began by introducing a curved seating area into the type of room used for noble entertainments. By the late 16th century they were putting up specially built indoor theaters. Next they separated the stage from the audience, setting it in a big frame, known as a *proscenium arch*. The first theater with a proscenium arch was built in 1619 in Parma, Italy.

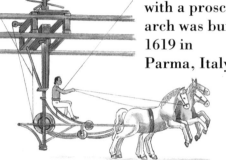

△ BEAMS AND WIRES lowered gods from the sky. The working parts of this chariot would be hidden by clouds, made of cloth that billowed. The horses probably had movable legs.

Changeable backgrounds were needed to suit the extravagant entertainments that audiences liked, and so the Italians also devised a system of sliding side panels, or *flats*, of painted canvas. These could change a seascape to a forest in a moment. The system was a huge success and was soon copied throughout Europe.

▽ THE STAGE was candlelit by chandeliers hanging from the proscenium arch.

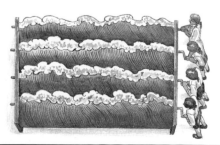

◁ THE EFFECT of a churning sea was achieved with a series of painted boards across the front of the stage. Each one dipped and tilted as a stagehand turned its handle.

▽ A REVOLVING scallop-shell throne from 1700. It was turned by two people crawling along.

22

◁ THESE SLIDING FLATS were used for a performance in Spain in 1652. The early sets were symmetrical, using perspective tricks to make the audience feel as if they were looking into an open space. By clever painting, flats could also suggest the sides of a room.

▽ OIL LAMPS, backed by reflectors, were used between the flats and across the front of the stage.

To be fashionable in the 17th and 18th centuries, it was essential to go to the theater. People sat in tiers of seats, in private compartments called boxes. Poorer people sat in benches in front of the stage, in an area known as the pit.

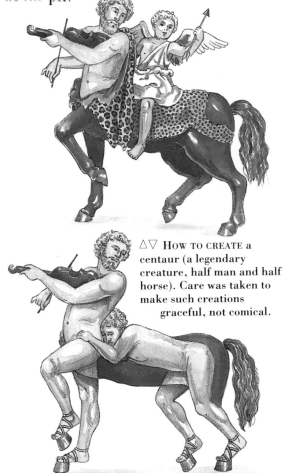

△▽ HOW TO CREATE a centaur (a legendary creature, half man and half horse). Care was taken to make such creations graceful, not comical.

△ THE SCHOUWBURG THEATER, Amsterdam, was originally opened in 1638, and rebuilt with a proscenium arch in 1665. On stage a hero rescues a heroine from a sea monster. The rocks are actually flats that are moved into place on rollers running along in grooves. The monster glides across the stage on a runway concealed by strips of mechanical waves. It moves its tail, jaws, and eyes when someone inside pulls its strings.

The use of boys for female roles ended in the 17th century when women began to appear on the stage. The acting was directed by the author or the theater owner. In the 19th century professional directors became responsible for the whole production. No one bothered much about historical accuracy until the 19th century, when great care was taken to get settings and costumes right.

OPERA

△ 17TH-CENTURY operatic performer. Louis XIV of France encouraged his court composer Lully to create operas.

▽ OUTDOOR OPERA, performed before Louis XIV in a courtyard at Versailles in 1674.

WHEN THE ITALIANS first attempted to recreate classical plays, they found that their noble audiences liked them to be enlivened with interludes of song and dance, even though these had little or nothing to do with the play. The interludes were so inventive that they became more popular than the plays themselves. By the 17th century a series of interludes, with sumptuous scene changes and stage effects, would be strung together to make an entire show. This type of entertainment was known as opera. It was performed at the courts of princes and quickly became popular with the upper classes. The first public opera house opened in Venice in 1637.

▷ THE PRESENT DAY Paris Opera House which was built for Napoleon III was opened in 1874.

▽ 18TH-CENTURY Venetian opera singers. Opera has always had a special place in the hearts of the Italians. In the 19th century, working people far too poor to afford a seat would be heard singing tunes from a recent first night.

Mozart.

The first operas were plays accompanied with music for voices and instruments, mixed with episodes of dancing. It needed a leap of imagination to realize that music, the art that most quickly touches our feelings, could be made to convey drama more vividly than words. The 17th-century Italian, Claudio Monteverdi, was the first composer to write emotionally expressive music for his characters, and his works are the first true operas. They are still performed today.

Opera remained an aristocratic entertainment in the 18th century; Mozart wrote for German princes. But by 1820 the middle classes appreciated opera.

▷ A 19TH-CENTURY souvenir plate showing La Scala, Milan's famous opera house, which opened in 1778. Cities competed with each other as centers of operatic excellence. La Scala holds a world position today.

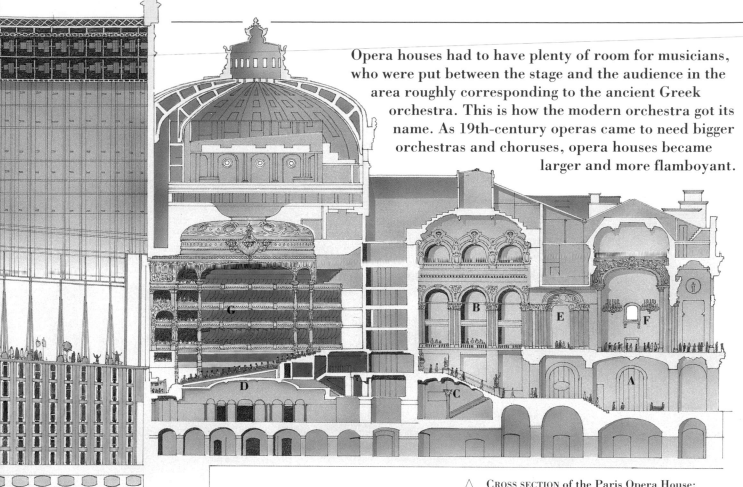

Opera houses had to have plenty of room for musicians, who were put between the stage and the audience in the area roughly corresponding to the ancient Greek orchestra. This is how the modern orchestra got its name. As 19th-century operas came to need bigger orchestras and choruses, opera houses became larger and more flamboyant.

△ CROSS SECTION of the Paris Opera House: A. entrance vestibule; B. grand staircase; C. decorative fountain; D. the Rotunda, a room set aside for people who paid subscriptions to the opera; E. lobby; F. main foyer; G. auditorium.

By the 19th century opera had split into comic opera and serious works, usually historical and tragical. Today, going to an opera is still regarded as a highbrow pastime, though enormous numbers of people are stirred by opera on television and will go to a recital when a great star sings the highlights.

Wagner.

GREAT COMPOSERS OF OPERA: the Austrian Mozart (*opposite page*), 1756-1791; the German Richard Wagner (*above*), 1813-1883; and the Italian Giuseppe Verdi (*below*), 1813-1901.

Verdi.

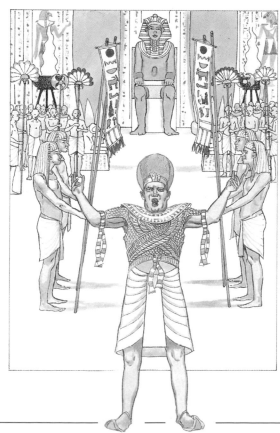

◁ A DRAMATIC MOMENT in Verdi's *Aida*. Verdi gave Italian opera, which had come to rely on trilling voices, a new vigor and emotional charge.

▷ LUCIANO PAVAROTTI, with Shirley Verret. Opera needs superlative singers. In opera houses their voices are not amplified.

BALLET

B ALLET, as we saw on page 21, developed from lavish court entertainments of the fifteenth and sixteenth centuries. Louis XIV founded the Académie Royale de Danse in 1661. His dancing master codified the positions of the feet. In the 18th century professional ballet dancers were strictly trained; by 1750 leaping and lifting movements were included in the techniques taught. Ballet spread throughout Europe and into Russia. In the 1830s "romantic" ballet, with wistful ballerinas in woodland glades, was devised to show off the graceful floating style of Marie Taglioni. Two American dancers, Isadora Duncan and Martha Graham, influenced the development of dance in the 20th century by breaking many of the strict ballet rules.

△ BALLET COSTUME, 1677. Only stately movement was possible in the tall headgear and stiff skirts of court ballet.

△ AN 18TH-CENTURY pas de deux. The costume is elaborate, but allows more leg movement.

△ THE GREAT RUSSIAN dancer and choreographer Nijinsky in *L'Après-midi d'un Faune*, created in 1912 for the Ballets Russes. This company thrilled Europe by its originality when it opened in Paris in 1909.

▽ ISADORA DUNCAN believed that dance should be a spontaneous expression of feeling.

△ MARIE CAMARGO, the most celebrated French ballerina of the 18th century, from a portrait painted around 1730.

◁ THE FAMOUS Italian dancer Marie Taglioni was the first ballerina to dance on points and to wear a tutu in *La Sylphide* in 1832.

◁ THE BASIC POSITIONS of classical ballet. There are five positions of the feet in which all steps in classical ballet begin and end, with the legs turned out from the pelvis.

△ BALLET STYLES. *Above*, an arabesque in the Romantic style. The line of the limbs is soft and fluid. The gauzy tutu is calf-length.

△ THE SAME POSE in the classical style is strong and clear-cut, with the leg raised higher. The stiff tutu shows the leg positions.

△ IN THE MODERN style the pose is more gymnastic and extreme. Every body movement is clearly revealed by the dancer's leotard.

PUPPETS

DRAW A FACE on your fingertip, give it a voice and movement, and you have a primitive puppet – an "actor" made to fit a special part and entirely controlled by you. There are four types of puppet: glove puppets, which are hands in disguise; marionettes with jointed parts worked by strings from above; rod puppets moved from below by rods attached to head and limbs; and shadow puppets worked from behind a screen on which they cast moving shadows. Glove puppets grip things well, so are good for slapstick. Jointed puppets excel in fantasy: dancing chairs and tables, a character that juggles with its head – such things are easy in the puppet theater.

Eastern Europe has full-scale puppet theater companies that perform serious, often satirical plays. Western puppets are usually regarded as children's entertainment, although Jim Hensen's *Muppet Show* appealed to television viewers of all ages. Puppets suit television, which makes small "actors" visible to a large audience.

△ 19TH-CENTURY Sicilian marionette. Private marionette theaters amused the Italian aristocracy in the 18th century. Public shows, especially Sicilian presentations of Charlemagne's knights in bloodthirsty battles, were hugely popular in the 19th century.

▽ JAPANESE BUNRAKU rod puppets. Bunraku is a highly regarded art. Chikamatsu, Japan's great 17th-century playwright, wrote mainly for it. The figures are worked on stage by men shrouded in black.

△ JAVANESE SHADOW puppets made of leather. Puppetry, like all drama, originated in religious ritual. In ancient Egypt, images of gods moved and answered questions. Puppets were for adults, and in the Far East are still taken very seriously. In Java the puppet master is regarded as a priest and a wise man. His legendary stories teach young people the religious, moral, and historical traditions of their country.

▷ BRITAIN'S MR. PUNCH is descended from Pulcinella of the Commedia dell'Arte. He came as a marionette via France in the 17th century, was given a wife called Judy, and became a glove puppet around 1800.

MUSIC HALL & PANTO

△ THE "CANCAN" was all the rage in the 1890s. Its fluttering petticoats and high kicks began in the music halls of Paris.

▽ CROSS SECTION of a late 19th-century theater, showing the space taken up by scenery and its equipment.

▷ JUGGLERS AND trapeze artists were favorite attractions. This poster advertises an appearance by Japanese acrobats.

VARIETY THEATERS appeared in the 19th century. Their origin was in the custom of taverns or supper houses supplying free entertainment to encourage people to buy more drink. By the 1850s proprietors were setting up proper stages and charging entrance fees. Variety was certainly a good name for the new shows, which featured all sorts of short acts, mainly song and dance, comedy turns, and acrobatics. A master of ceremonies introduced each act and kept noisy customers in order. The first audiences were working men, but from the 1870s a successful effort was made to attract the upper classes. Large variety theaters were built, and food and drink were no longer served at the tables in the auditorium. Leading music hall stars were adored by the public.

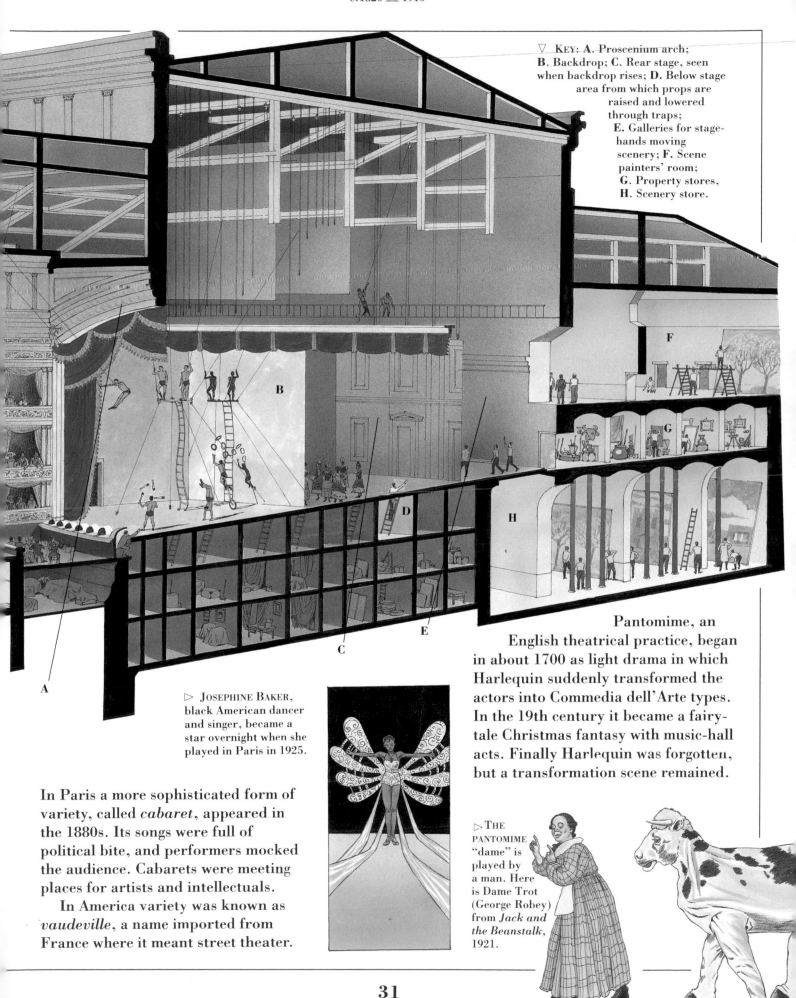

▽ KEY: **A.** Proscenium arch;
B. Backdrop; **C.** Rear stage, seen
when backdrop rises; **D.** Below stage
area from which props are
raised and lowered
through traps;
E. Galleries for stagehands moving
scenery; **F.** Scene
painters' room;
G. Property stores,
H. Scenery store.

▷ JOSEPHINE BAKER,
black American dancer
and singer, became a
star overnight when she
played in Paris in 1925.

In Paris a more sophisticated form of
variety, called *cabaret*, appeared in
the 1880s. Its songs were full of
political bite, and performers mocked
the audience. Cabarets were meeting
places for artists and intellectuals.

In America variety was known as
vaudeville, a name imported from
France where it meant street theater.

Pantomime, an
English theatrical practice, began
in about 1700 as light drama in which
Harlequin suddenly transformed the
actors into Commedia dell'Arte types.
In the 19th century it became a fairy-
tale Christmas fantasy with music-hall
acts. Finally Harlequin was forgotten,
but a transformation scene remained.

▷ THE
PANTOMIME
"dame" is
played by
a man. Here
is Dame Trot
(George Robey)
from *Jack and
the Beanstalk*,
1921.

THE AGE OF CINEMA

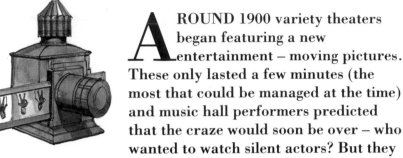

△ ▷ MAGIC LANTERN shows date from the 17th century. The lantern (*right*) shines a beam through a painted glass slide and a lens, to project an enlarged image onto a screen.

AROUND 1900 variety theaters began featuring a new entertainment – moving pictures. These only lasted a few minutes (the most that could be managed at the time) and music hall performers predicted that the craze would soon be over – who wanted to watch silent actors? But they were wrong. It was the music halls that were forced to close in the end.

It all began in 1824 when the principle known as *persistence of vision* was being experimented with. It was discovered that the brain holds the image that the eye sends it for a split second longer than the eye actually registers it. If the eye sends separate images rapidly enough, they overlap in the brain and we see what appears to be a single moving picture. The first moving pictures were made by toys in which a spinning series of drawn images suggested movement. But, in the 1870s the Englishman Eadweard Muybridge devised a means of taking split-second photographs in rapid succession, and lifelike moving pictures became possible. The films we watch today are no more than a series of still photographs shown at high speed.

△ THE FANTASMAGORIE, 1800. Images were made to loom and shrink, by moving the magic lantern backward and forward rapidly.

△ ▷ THIS TOY of 1826 uses the principle of merging images in the brain. Twirl the disc and the gladiator on one side fights the lion on the other.

▽ A GIRL VIEWS an 1876 praxinoscope. The images are inside a spinning drum and she watches their reflection in a mirror.

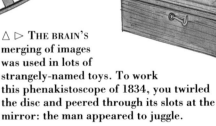

△ ▷ THE BRAIN'S merging of images was used in lots of strangely-named toys. To work this phenakistoscope of 1834, you twirled the disc and peered through its slots at the mirror: the man appeared to juggle.

◁ △ THE ZOOPRAXISCOPE, 1882, used painted versions of Muybridge's action photographs viewed through slots, to show truly lifelike movement.

◁ THE KINETOSCOPE, developed by Thomas Edison in 1891, was a slot machine showing a film lasting 15 seconds. It is shown open to reveal the mechanism that turns the loop of film. The picture was viewed through a peephole at the top. People lined up to watch.

△ POSTER FOR the world's first public film show in Paris in 1895, given by the Lumière brothers. Only 35 people turned up on the first day, but soon cinemas were a runaway success.

△ GEORGE SMITH (seen here crouching in front of the camera) was a pioneer filmmaker in Brighton, England. He built his 1900 studio in a greenhouse, for filming in all kinds of weather. Before this, films were shot outdoors, because artificial lighting was costly. Indoor scenes (which had actually been filmed outdoors) often showed clothes and tablecloths fluttering in the wind!

▷ FILM was first used for motion photography in the 1890s. These shots show one of film's most celebrated comics, Charlie Chaplin, who was a music hall clown at the age of eight and created his famous "Tramp" in 1914.

Two further things were needed before moving pictures could really begin to be a big success: a means of taking a vast number of photographs continuously and a way of showing them to a big audience. The invention of photographic film in rolls solved the first problem, and the old magic lantern technique of projection onto a screen solved the second.

After 1905 small motion picture theaters sprang up all over Europe and America. In the States they were called *nickelodeons*, because you originally paid a nickel to get in. A program usually had six ten-minute films, including a comedy, a melodrama, and a chase.

△ IDOLS of the silent screen: shy comedian Harold Lloyd; Rudolph Valentino, the great lover; John Gilbert, a manly hero; Lillian Gish, a popular actress.

33

THE RADIO

ON CHRISTMAS EVE 1906 ships' wireless operators in the Atlantic were astonished when they heard music and voices coming out of their sets. Until then the wireless, the name given by Marconi to his invention of communication by electro-magnetic waves, had sent messages only as morse-code bleeps. What the wireless operators heard was the very first radio broadcast of a phonograph recording. It was sent out by a Canadian scientist, R.A. Fessenden.

During the First World War radio transmission improved, and the first public broadcast was made in 1920. Independent radio stations opened all over the United States and Europe.

The radio revolutionized entertainment. Although television has since overshadowed the radio, at the time the novelty of being able to listen to news, comedy shows, talk shows, and plays in the home was amazing.

△ A MARCONI RADIO of the late 1920s, with built-in loudspeaker. Earphones attached to the set were no longer needed.

△ "NATION SHALL speak peace unto nation" was the motto of the BBC, an ideal that the BBC World Service has done its best to promote.

▽ A FAMILY IN THE 1940s. The radio was listened to attentively, and not treated as background noise for other activities.

△ UNTIL THE LATE 1930s, male announcers on BBC Radio were expected to wear tuxedos when broadcasting.

△ DANCING to the radio, 1920s. This wind-up portable radio is the size of a suitcase and must have been brought along by car.

▽ DANCING to the radio, 1950s. The music is coming from a high-fidelity console – an attractive piece of furniture housing a radio and record player.

▷ 1958 PORTABLE radio. For many years radios were hefty because of bulky vacuum tubes. This changed in the 1950s when the tubes were replaced by tiny transistors, invented in 1947.

THE MUSICAL

IN THE EARLY 20TH CENTURY, musical comedy was a lighthearted type of play with song and dance. The Americans adapted the formula in the 1920s into a more powerful drama with a strong musical focus. Some works, such as George Gershwin's 1935 *Porgy and Bess*, treated character and plot too seriously to be called comedy, and musical became the accepted term.

When the talkies arrived (see pages 36 and 37) they provided a natural vehicle for song and dance, creating a special type of film, the film musical. In the 1930s highly polished films such as Busby Berkeley's chorus spectaculars and the Fred Astaire/Ginger Rogers song-and-dance romances delighted worldwide audiences. Successful stage musicals – *Oklahoma*, 1943, *My Fair Lady*, 1956, and many others since – have been turned into films.

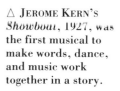

△ JEROME KERN'S *Showboat*, 1927, was the first musical to make words, dance, and music work together in a story.

▽ GANG FIGHT dance from Leonard Bernstein's *West Side Story*, 1957, a powerful reworking of the Romeo and Juliet story.

△ FRED ASTAIRE (*top of page*) in *Top Hat*, 1935, and Julie Andrews (*above*) in *The Sound of Music*, 1964. Both films were box office hits.

◁ JOHN TRAVOLTA in *Saturday Night Fever*, a popular film musical released in 1977.

▷ STARS OF INDIA'S giant musical-making industry. Most Indian films are lavish musical romances.

◁ THE ROCK musical *Hair* opened in London in 1968, the day after the abolition of British stage censorship, which had been in force since the 17th century. The musical celebrated the ideals of the 1960s – peace, love, and freedom. During the show the cast stripped naked. Though the lights dimmed, some people were shocked.

▽ IN THE 1960s rock music was first used in stage musicals. Andrew Lloyd Webber had huge successes with a new type of musical called rock opera. Here is a scene from *Phantom of the Opera*, 1986.

THE TALKIES

▷ POSTER for *The Jazz Singer*, 1927, the first full-length film to have its own sound. Some of the film was silent, but Jolson suddenly burst into song. *Lights of New York*, 1928, was the first complete "talkie."

ALTHOUGH EXPERIMENTS in producing sound movies had been going on since the beginning of the century, the film industry was lukewarm about them. Films were expensive to make and companies wanted to be sure of getting their money back. Silent films were a success world-wide because they used mime to convey meaning. Their few brief captions were cheap to translate for foreign distribution. Film studios feared the overseas market might collapse overnight if audiences heard their screen idols speaking in a language they could not understand. Eventually the film company Warner Brothers took the risk and proved the doubters wrong. One of Al Jolson's lines in their epoch-making film *The Jazz Singer* was the catchphrase: "You ain't heard nothin' yet!" Other film companies got the message and the race was on to get into the market for "talkies."

△ THE FIRST sound projector ran the spool of film separately from the sound disc. There was a risk of the wrong disc being played accidentally.

△ THE ODEON, Leicester Square, London, a typical cinema of the 1930s. They were so lavishly decorated that they were called "picture palaces."

▷ A BOOM MICROPHONE. The long pole, or *boom*, is able to follow the actors around the set but keep out of the shot. The first microphones were hidden on the set and the actors had to stay close to them, which hampered their movements.

△ FILM that carried both sound and image was a great advance over the disc and spool, which could get out of sync with each other. A tube in the camera reacted to sound levels by giving off light of varying intensity, and this was recorded as a track of lines along the film. A light-sensitive cell in the projector read the lines and turned them back into sound.

▽ PROPAGANDA films sway people more than thousands of words. The Soviet government created a movie-train that took propaganda shows to every corner of the USSR.

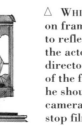

△ WHITE CANVAS on frames is used to reflect light onto the actors. The director is in charge of the film crew. When he shouts "Cut," the cameraman will stop filming.

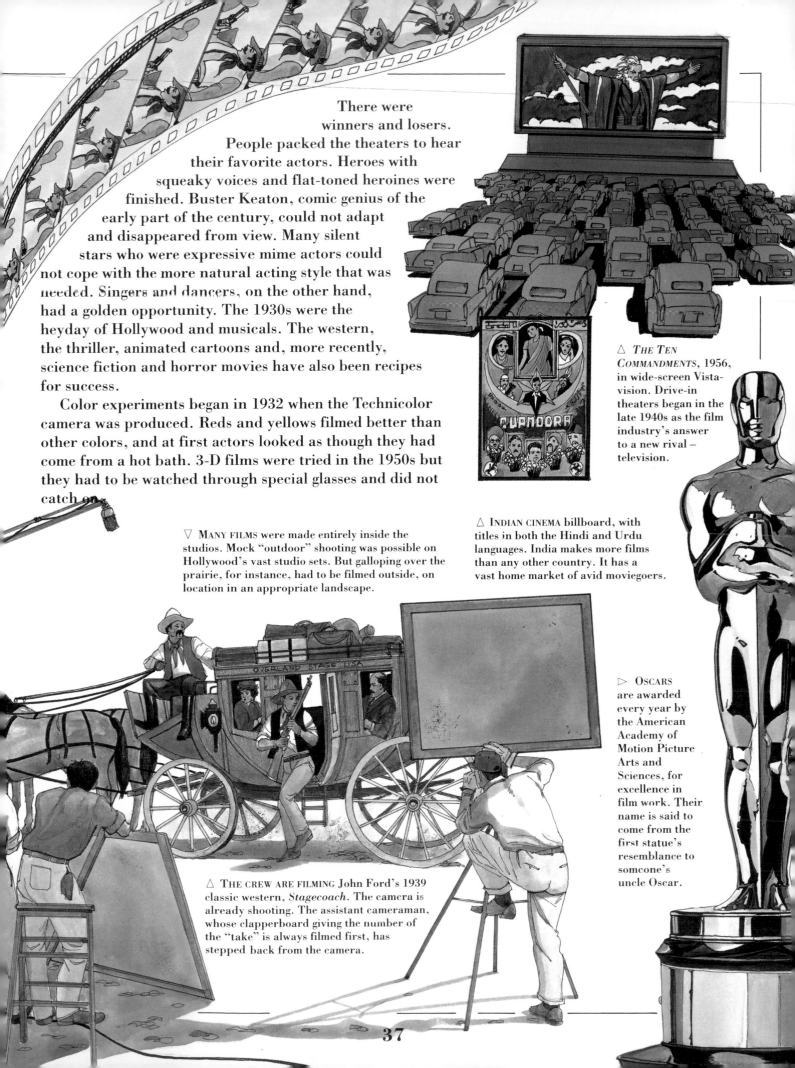

There were winners and losers. People packed the theaters to hear their favorite actors. Heroes with squeaky voices and flat-toned heroines were finished. Buster Keaton, comic genius of the early part of the century, could not adapt and disappeared from view. Many silent stars who were expressive mime actors could not cope with the more natural acting style that was needed. Singers and dancers, on the other hand, had a golden opportunity. The 1930s were the heyday of Hollywood and musicals. The western, the thriller, animated cartoons and, more recently, science fiction and horror movies have also been recipes for success.

Color experiments began in 1932 when the Technicolor camera was produced. Reds and yellows filmed better than other colors, and at first actors looked as though they had come from a hot bath. 3-D films were tried in the 1950s but they had to be watched through special glasses and did not catch on.

△ *The Ten Commandments*, 1956, in wide-screen Vista-vision. Drive-in theaters began in the late 1940s as the film industry's answer to a new rival – television.

△ Indian cinema billboard, with titles in both the Hindi and Urdu languages. India makes more films than any other country. It has a vast home market of avid moviegoers.

▽ Many films were made entirely inside the studios. Mock "outdoor" shooting was possible on Hollywood's vast studio sets. But galloping over the prairie, for instance, had to be filmed outside, on location in an appropriate landscape.

△ The crew are filming John Ford's 1939 classic western, *Stagecoach*. The camera is already shooting. The assistant cameraman, whose clapperboard giving the number of the "take" is always filmed first, has stepped back from the camera.

▷ Oscars are awarded every year by the American Academy of Motion Picture Arts and Sciences, for excellence in film work. Their name is said to come from the first statue's resemblance to someone's uncle Oscar.

△ ONE OF THE FIRST TV pictures transmitted on Baird's equipment.

△ 1935 TV SET, cut away to show the cathode ray tube, the radio receiver and the loudspeaker.

◁ THE BBC's Alexandra Palace studio, London, from which the first public television broadcast was made in 1936.

TELEVISION

FROM THE FIRST DIM picture transmitted in 1925 by the Scotsman John Logie Baird, television has mushroomed to become the world's favorite entertainment, bringing action into homes at the touch of a button. Like radio it is sent out as electronic signals, that sets convert into sounds and pictures. The device that made this possible was the electronic scanner developed in the 1920s. Both Britain and the United States were experimenting with television in the 1930s. The BBC (British Broadcasting Corporation) started the first public service in 1936. Only two separate hour-long transmissions went out each day. It was believed that viewers would grow fatigued watching television for more than two hours! The cost of sets – around $500, quite expensive then – made prewar viewing a treat for the rich.

After the Second World War black-and-white broadcasting developed rapidly in the United States, England, France, and Germany. Color television developed in the United States during the late 1940s.

Today there are tiny portable TVs using liquid crystal displays and video cassette recorders that let us watch one program while recording another. And with a video camera we can even put ourselves on the screen.

△ THE MARCONIPHONE TV of 1937 showed you the screen reflected in the lid, which you shut afterward.

△ THESE BOYS are able to watch the 1948 London Olympics on their father's home-built "Green Screen Wonder."

▽ TV SETS come in all shapes and sizes. *Below*, an unusual spherical model from the 1970s. The globe can be rotated for viewing from any angle.

◁ NEWS that the Queen's coronation would be televised gave sales of sets in Britain a huge boost in 1953.

△ COLOR was common by the 1960s. The signal is separated into three beams that scan phosphorus dots on the screen. Each picks out dots that will glow with a corresponding color – red, green, or blue.

▷ A VIDEO CASSETTE stores TV pictures on magnetic tape. Magnetic particles record images in a series of diagonal tracks, making it possible to pack in huge amounts of information.

JAZZ, ROCK & POP

POPULAR MUSIC – an umbrella term covering a wealth of sounds – is a phenomenon of the 20th century. Through records and radio the world was suddenly able to share music, and its development therefore began to reflect mass opinion. The sounds that caused the most excitement came from black America.

△ THE GREAT JAZZ SOLOIST Louis Armstrong (1901-1971), famous for his magnificent trumpet playing.

△ PARAMOUNT record of the early 1930s. Record companies rushed to record the Big Band sound of bandleaders like Duke Ellington and Glenn Miller.

▷ BESSIE SMITH (1894-1937), one of the first great jazz singers, unmatched in the 1920s for powerful blues.

▷ JIVING in the 1950s. The Jive was an improvised dance involving lots of rapid swings, lifts, and turns. It was a wilder form of the jitterbug popular in the swing era of the 1930s and 1940s.

▷ ELVIS PRESLEY grew up listening to rhythm and blues on black radio stations, and started the teen revolution of the 1950s with "Heartbreak Hotel," "Blue Suede Shoes," and "Hound Dog" for RCA in 1956.

▽ THE BEATLES, the English group who transformed rock 'n' roll with their first big success, "Please Please Me" in 1963.

George Harrison.

Ringo Starr.

John Lennon.

The first mass popular music was jazz, born from the folk music of the black slaves. Ragtime, a type of jazz, was a jaunty piano style that emerged from St. Louis and spread across the western world at the turn of the century. Then came blues, developed from the call-and-response singing patterns that black field hands remembered from their African ancestors. The skill of the accompanying musicians was expressed in brilliant improvisations.

As black workers moved north to industrial cities like Chicago, jazz developed a tougher, more driving style, called rhythm and blues. From the 1940s it was played on electric guitars with bass and drum backing.

△ BUDDY HOLLY (1936-1959), an original rock 'n' roller, killed in mid-career in a plane crash.

▽ ALAN FREED fan. Freed, a white DJ, played black rhythm and blues in 1952, calling it "rock 'n' roll."

Paul McCartney.

Jazz, in a diluted form, became the white dance music of the 1920s. In the 1930s, played by big bands with large brass sections, it was known as swing. The only genuinely white tradition to flourish alongside jazz in the 1930s was the country and western music of traveling folksingers.

After the Second World War American teenagers were looking for a new sound. Big band jazz was over; crooners like Frank Sinatra and Bing Crosby seemed middle-aged. Suddenly, in the 1950s, there was rock 'n' roll, in which the drive of rhythm and blues was grafted onto country and western music.

After Elvis the pop scene took off. In the 1960s the Beatles pioneered the acceptable side of rock, the Rolling Stones were its bad boys, and Bob Dylan gave it political commitment. The 1970s brought punk rock, glam rock and disco. Since then reggae, rap, heavy metal and house music have made their mark, each with a separate stance and style.

△ BEATLES' BADGES. Merchandising spin-offs like fan clubs, posters, magazines, badges, and T-shirts can earn pop stars a considerable amount of money, although what percentage of the proceeds they receive will depend on their individual contracts.

△ 1960s PSYCHEDELIC imagery used in an advertisement for a stereo car radio.

▷ JIMI HENDRIX (1942-1970), one of rock's most brilliant guitarists, burst onto the music scene in 1967. His style was wild and musically very inventive.

△ BOB MARLEY (1945-1981) gave the world reggae, the music of Jamaica's poorest blacks. Marley sang of black idealism: love, peace, and freedom.

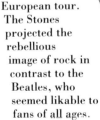

▷ MICK JAGGER, lead singer of the Rolling Stones, at the band's 1972 European tour. The Stones projected the rebellious image of rock in contrast to the Beatles, who seemed likable to fans of all ages.

◁ 1970s PUNK with Sex Pistols T-shirt. Punk rock represented the rejection of conventional values. Punk clothes, appearance, and music set out to offend, shock, and disrupt society.

◁ PUNK ACCESSORIES were deliberately outrageous: safety pins pierced through flesh, razor blades on chains, and death's head badges.

△ HELPING CHARITY. David Bowie, Paul McCartney and Bob Geldof performing at the Live Aid Concert in 1985.

▽ POPULAR ROCK BANDS can attract huge audiences to arenas such as Wembley in London.

ENTERTAINMENT TODAY

TODAY WE CAN CHOOSE all sorts of entertainment without even leaving our living rooms. We can select from hundreds of TV channels on a screen that will soon rival the cinema's, while we record something else to watch later. We can see the latest films on laser disc, which gives better sound and pictures than ever before. Satellites receive signals from the opposite side of the earth and bounce them instantly into our homes so that we can watch sporting events and hear concerts at the moment they are taking place in the farthest corners of the world.

If we feel like going out we can take our entertainment with us wherever we are with a personal stereo and pocket computer game player. If real life is boring we can swap it for a more interesting version through virtual reality, which uses computer graphics to make it seem as though we are actually part of the scene we are watching.

△ WIDE-SCREEN TV sets are as yet available only in Japan, which has the digital system for High Definition Television.

▷ KARAOKE was the brainchild of the Japanese record industry. Sing along to a backing track and imagine that you are a pop star.

◁ A LASER DISC carries visual information and sound in digital form, which is read by a laser beam. It is set to take over from the video cassette. We will soon have the digital compact cassette, and a mini disc which will record pictures and sound together.

Very soon, manufacturers promise, the TV picture will be super sharp and extra bright, made up of 1,250 flicker-free lines. We shall be able to back-project it onto a wall of our room. Already, thanks to synthesizers and mixers, we can listen to music made of sounds never heard or imagined before, from instruments and singers that do not really exist.

▽ A HAND-HELD computer game. Micro-processors containing microchip technology enable miniature computers like this to be made quite cheaply. The first commercial video game was invented in 1972.

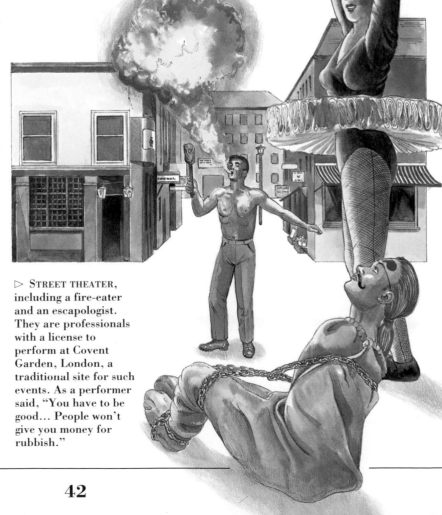

▷ STREET THEATER, including a fire-eater and an escapologist. They are professionals with a license to perform at Covent Garden, London, a traditional site for such events. As a performer said, "You have to be good… People won't give you money for rubbish."

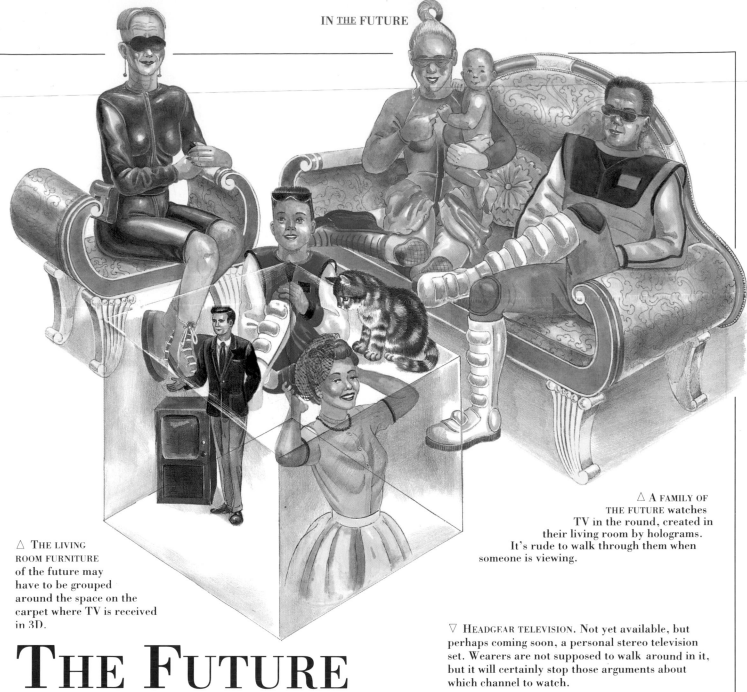

△ THE LIVING
ROOM FURNITURE
of the future may
have to be grouped
around the space on the
carpet where TV is received
in 3D.

△ A FAMILY OF
THE FUTURE watches
TV in the round, created in
their living room by holograms.
It's rude to walk through them when
someone is viewing.

▽ HEADGEAR TELEVISION. Not yet available, but
perhaps coming soon, a personal stereo television
set. Wearers are not supposed to walk around in it,
but it will certainly stop those arguments about
which channel to watch.

THE FUTURE

W HAT NEXT? Hologram TV perhaps, or a mini-set
to strap across our eyes as we travel on public
transportation or wait in line in the supermarket.
Maybe an entertainment pill, taken at bedtime, will give us
the video of our choice while we sleep, in place of old-
fashioned dreams.

But wait a minute. Aren't we forgetting something?
Technology can bring us entertainment in new ways, but it
cannot guarantee us more enjoyment. That still depends on
the quality of the performance. Watch a street entertainer, a
juggler perhaps, doing an act that was old when the Romans
watched it. Passersby gather around. They love it. They
laugh and applaud. It's real and it's being done just for
them. That's entertainment.

TIMELINE

Dancing jesters, c.1340

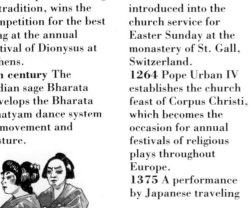

Tribal dance,
Papua New Guinea

B.C.
c.2300 A papyrus of this date in the British Museum recounts a religious ceremony in which priests act the parts of gods.
c.1400 Ancient Egyptian wall paintings depict professional dancing girls and musicians performing at private banquets.
c.1000 Hindu temple rituals include drama.

Processional wagon

c.1000 The ancient Greeks honor Dionysus, god of wine and fertility, in a festival of wild dancing. During the following centuries dance-drama becomes part of agricultural festivals.
6th century The festivities for Dionysus have become a formal performance of dancing and song, by a chorus of 50 men.
534 Thespis, according to tradition, wins the competition for the best song at the annual festival of Dionysus at Athens.
5th century The Indian sage Bharata develops the Bharata Nhatyam dance system of movement and gesture.

Japanese Kabuki actors

486 Comedy is established at the Athenian festival of Dionysus. The great Greek dramatists, Aeschylus, Sophocles, and Euripides, are writing in this century.
3rd century Indian drama reaches China.
264 Gladiator combats become a feature of the Roman games.
c.55 The first public theater in Pompeii is built.

A.D.
c.80 The Colosseum, Rome's amphitheater, is opened.

312 The Roman Emperor Constantine is converted to Christianity. Laws are passed banning cruel entertainments.
410 Roman theaters are closed after the sack of Rome by Alaric the Visigoth.
c.720 The Chinese Emperor Ming Huang opens the Pear Garden training school for actors.
975 Drama is introduced into the church service for Easter Sunday at the monastery of St. Gall, Switzerland.
1264 Pope Urban IV establishes the church feast of Corpus Christi, which becomes the occasion for annual festivals of religious plays throughout Europe.
1375 A performance by Japanese traveling

players Kanami and his son Zeami impresses the Shogun (military head of government). He takes them into his service and Noh drama is established.
c.1400 Zeami writes *Kadensho* (The Handing Down of the Flower), a discussion of the theory of Noh.
1418 Mumming is banned in London.
1486 The earliest classical revival, the ancient Roman comedy, *Menaechmi*, by Plautus, is staged in Ferrara, Italy.
c.1550 Formation of the first Commedia dell'Arte companies.
1576 The Gelosi company of Commedia dell'Arte players visit Paris. They are soon followed by others.
1579 First public theater in Spain opens in Madrid. Playwrights Lope de Vega (1562-1635) and Calderon (1600-81) create the golden age of Spanish drama.

15th-century wood-carving, "Christ and the Moneylenders"

1581 *The Ballet Comique de la Royne,* the first dance entertainment to tell a story, is performed at the French court.
1585 The Teatro Olimpico in Vicenza, Italy, the oldest surviving Renaissance theater, is opened.
1599 *Dafne*, the first opera, is performed in Florence.
1598 The Globe Theater is built. It is burned down in 1613.

c.1600 Kathakali dance-drama originates in temples of the southern province of Kerala in India.
1607 Monteverdi's opera *Orfeo* produced in Mantua, Italy.
1616 Death of Shakespeare.

William Shakespeare

1619 The Teatro Farnese in Parma, Italy, is the first theater to be built with a proscenium opening framing the stage.
c.1620 Flats sliding in grooves are introduced to create easily changeable stage scenery.
1637 First public opera house, the Teatro San Cassiano, opens in Venice.
1641 Giacomo Torelli invents an improved system of flats inserted through slots in the stage and running on trolleys underneath it.

c.1659 Dutch scientist Christiaan Huygens invents the magic lantern to project medical pictures.
1662 An Italian showman presents Pulcinella, the forerunner of Punch, in a booth in Covent Garden, London.
1669 Louis XIV founds the Académie Royale de Musique. French dramatists Corneille, Molière, and Racine are writing.

Algerian street musicians

1680 The Commedia dell'Arte opens its own permanent theater at Hôtel de Bourgogne, Paris. In 1697 its humor offends Mme de Maintenon (secret wife of Louis XIV), and the theater is closed.
1681 Death of the great Spanish playwright Calderon.
1733 The first comic opera, *La Serva Padrona* by Pergolesi, is performed in Italy.
1768 Philip Astley opens his Riding School, the first circus.

Indian Kathak performers, 1398

1789 *La Fille Mal Gardée*, a French ballet, is performed. It is the oldest ballet still regularly danced today.

c.1800 Belgian illusionist Etienne Gaspard Robertson invents the Fantasmagorie.

1858 Napoleon III decides to build a new Paris opera house. Work begins in 1861 and takes 14 years.

1872-8 Eadweard Muybridge devises a way of taking photographs in rapid succession, in order to settle a bet as to whether a galloping horse lifts all its feet off the ground at once. This was the beginning of films.

How to create a centaur

1825 The principle of *persistence of vision* is announced to the Royal Society in London by P.M. Roget.

1832 Marie Taglioni, dancing in *La Sylphide*, wears the now traditional ballet tutu, points, and pink tights for the first time on stage.

1874 Circus elephants appear for the first time in Howe's Great London Circus.

1877 American Thomas Edison invents the phonograph, which plays recordings made on tinfoil cylinders.

Stage scenery from Spain, 1652

1841 *Giselle*, the essence of romantic ballet, is performed at the Paris Opera.

1854-74 Wagner composes *The Ring of the Nibelung*.

1880 The gramophone, which plays recordings on disks, appears.

1887 A motion picture camera is patented by Thomas Edison.

1889 Celluloid photographic film marketed by American George Eastman, the founder of Kodak.

1895 The first public film show is given in the basement of a Paris café by Louis and Auguste Lumière.

1896 Guglielmo Marconi patents his invention of radio communication.

1899 "Maple Leaf Rag" earns American composer and pianist Scott Joplin the title of "King of Ragtime."

1909 Serge Diaghilev's company the Ballets Russes founded in Paris.

1910 American radio pioneer Lee de Forest broadcasts the famous tenor Enrico Caruso singing live from the Metropolitan Opera House, New York.

1917 An early jazz recording is made in New York by The Original Dixieland Jass Band.

1922 The first regular radio broadcasts are made in America and Britain.

1923 The BBC is licensed to broadcast.

1923 King Oliver's Creole Jazz Band makes the first black jazz recording.

1925 Josephine Baker appears in La Revue Nègre in Paris and becomes a star overnight.

1926 German director Fritz Lang produces the futuristic silent movie *Metropolis*.

1927 Valve radio sets with loudspeakers appear, replacing crystal sets and earphones.

1927 Al Jolson appears in the first "talkie."

1928 Development of an electronic scanning device, the iconoscope, by Russian-born American Vladimir Kosma Zworykin, improves television technology.

1930 The first broadcast to be heard worldwide, George V's speech to a naval conference, is transmitted.

1932 The BBC begins shortwave transmissions (for long-distance broadcasting) in foreign languages.

Film idols, 1920s

1933 Fred Astaire and Ginger Rogers begin their film partnership with *Flying Down to Rio*.

1935 George Gershwin's *Porgy and Bess* is the first musical acted by a black cast.

1939 The first screening of *The Wizard of Oz* – the most famous and successful family film musical.

Phenakistoscope, 1831

1953 Coronation of Queen Elizabeth II is televised.

1954 Bill Hayley records "Rock around the Clock."

1958 The musical *West Side Story* is performed in London.

1960s Stereophonic broadcasting begins.

1963 Beatlemania takes Britain and America by storm.

1969 Woodstock rock festival attracts 500,000 fans in New York State.

1969 Video cassettes introduced from Japan by Sony.

1970 The emergence of the mass-market pop video to promote bands and their music.

1978 Pacman computer game heralds the beginning of a new age in computer entertainment.

1979 Sony Walkman personal stereo introduced.

1983 Compact discs begin to replace LPs.

1983 Cable television begins to appear in Great Britain.

1987 Digital audio tape systems available.

1988 Development of satellite dish for domestic use.

1989 Virtual reality interactive computer games introduced.

1990 Invention of the Sony Discman.

1991 Gameboy hand-held computer game is voted most popular toy in the United States and Britain.

Karaoke

GLOSSARY

Apartheid South African laws forcing blacks and whites to live separately.

Arabesque Ballet position in which the dancer stands on one leg, with the other leg raised behind.

Calypso A musical style of West Indian origin, influenced by jazz, usually having topical, often improvised, lyrics.

Capstan Drum turned by projections, which winds or unwinds a rope.

Caste A social class or system based on distinctions of wealth, heredity, or rank.

Cathode ray tube Electron tube in a TV set that provides the picture.

Colonnade A row of identical columns, often surrounding a courtyard.

Dark Ages The period from the fall of the Roman Empire to the beginning of the Middle Ages, roughly the 5th to 10th centuries A.D.

Digital Using information supplied in the form of numbers.

Escapologist An entertainer who escapes from bonds or from a container apparently impossible to untie or open.

Farce Comedy that relies on ludicrous characters and situations.

Flemish From an area, of which Flanders was the largest province, corresponding to modern Belgium.

Float A large wheeled platform, usually part of a procession or parade.

Guild An association of craftsmen belonging to the same trade.

Hindu Belonging to, or believing in, Hinduism, the religion of 85 percent of India's population.

Hologram A three-dimensional image created by laser beams.

Jester A professional joker or "fool," permanently employed to amuse royalty or nobles, in times when there was little entertainment.

Laser An intense beam of single-wavelength light. A laser disc holds information read by a laser beam.

Leotard A close-fitting one-piece garment with long sleeves and legs, invented in the 19th century by the French gymnast Leotard.

Liquid crystal display Images which are made by changes in the pattern of reflected light from a layer of liquid crystal (a semi-melted mineral).

Mansion In medieval times, a small stage or setting. Several would be grouped in the space in which a play was acted. The actors moved from one to the next, to indicate a change of place.

Melodrama A drama which plays heavily on the audience's emotions, but has a happy ending.

Mime Using body movements and facial expressions to convey actions or emotions without the use of speech.

Miniature A very small painting, usually a portrait.

Mongol invasions The expansion of the Mongol tribes of central Asia. They established an empire which extended from China to eastern Europe and were at the height of their power in the 13th century A.D.

Nave The main part of the interior of a church, separated from the aisles by pillars.

Orchestra Circular area in a Greek theater, in which the chorus performed.

Pagan Follower of polytheistic religion (one that worships many gods).

Pageant A movable stage setting on wheels.

Pantomime Using body movements and facial expressions to express actions or emotions without the use of speech. It originated in ancient Rome.

Phosphorus A chemical that gives off light when exposed to the air.

Points The toe-blocks in ballet shoes that help the dancer to balance.

Projection The throwing of light or sound as used in motion pictures.

Projectionist Cinema technician responsible for projecting the film onto the screen.

Proscenium The area in front of the *skene* (a long low building used by the actors) in a Greek theater. From the 17th century, the arch framing the stage in a European theater.

Psychedelic Producing an abnormal mental state in which distorted images or hallucinations may be experienced.

Sampler A computer that can record, modify, and reproduce any form of sound.

Satyric A type of Greek play involving satyrs – woodland gods who looked like humans with horses' ears and tails.

Shawm A double-reeded woodwind instrument.

Slapstick Knock-about comedy.

Soul music A musical style inspired by the gospel singing of black American churchgoers.

Stereophonic Broadcasting of sound through separate channels to two or more loudspeakers.

Subscriptions Regular payments made by the supporters of a theater to help it financially.

Synthesizer An instrument that creates and modifies sounds electronically. It produces artificial sounds that are similar to those of particular musical instruments.

The three Marys Mary, mother of Christ, Mary Magdalene, and Mary, mother of James the apostle.

Transistor A small electronic device that switches the flow of electrical current between two terminals.

Troupe A small company of performers.

Tutu The short stiff skirt of a ballerina.

Winch A horizontal drum around which a rope is wound. It is turned by a handle to wind or unwind the rope.

INDEX